JULIAN

J. Janda

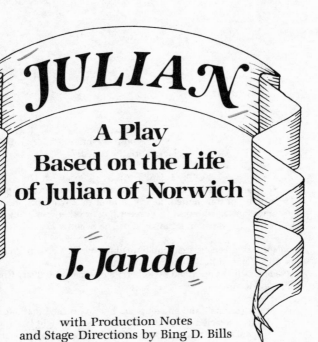

JULIAN

A Play Based on the Life of Julian of Norwich

J. Janda

with Production Notes
and Stage Directions by Bing D. Bills

Illustrations by
William Hart McNichols

A Vineyard Book

The Seabury Press / New York

The Seabury Press
815 Second Avenue
New York, N.Y. 10017

Julian was given its first public reading by Sr. Carolyn Weithorn at St.
Joseph's Convent in Baden, Pennsylvania.
Julian was first performed by Roberta Nobleman at Calvary Church, Sum-
mit, New Jersey.

Printed in the United States of America

Library of Congress Cataloging in Publication Data

Janda, J. (James), 1936-
Julian: a play based on the life of Julian of Norwich.

1. Julian, of Norwich, b. 1343—Drama.   I. Title.
PS3560.A45J8   1984   812'.54   83-20030
ISBN 0-8164-2632-5 (pbk.)

For Roberta, Bing, Jean, Billie, A.B.
and all who helped bring *Julian* to
a larger audience.

Other works by J. Janda

Poetry
Hanbelachia
Nobody Stop by to See

Plays
That Sacred Hunger
By Children Deceived
Voices
La calavera y la mariposa

JULIAN OF NORWICH: (b. 1342, d. 1415?) woman, mystic, recluse, spiritual guide, author of *Revelations of Divine Love;* survived three outbreaks of the Black Plague that reduced the population of England by half; survived the Peasants' Revolt, the Great Western Schism, the Hundred Years' War; wrote of God as mother, as courteous, as all-loving, as all-forgiving.

Acknowledgments

Grateful acknowledgment is hereby made for permission to quote from *Revelations of Divine Love* by Julian of Norwich, edited by Dom Roger Huddleston (London: Burns, Oates, and Washbourne, 1927). These quotations are identified in the text by a dagger (†).

The quotations from *The Nun's Rule,* edited by James Morton (St. Louis: B. Herder, 1905), are identified in the text by an asterisk (*).

Simeon's prayer is from Luke 2:29–32, Authorized (King James) Version.

Production Notes

J. Janda's *Julian* is susceptible to a variety of staging possibilities. Certainly as a poem celebrating the life and love of Julian, it is more than complete. For those who might wish to stage it, the directions in this text represent one particular approach.

One rule has dictated directorial comments: the simpler the better, so that the words of Julian and Janda remain dominant.

SETTING

Julian's room consists of a bed, a chest, an altar, and two small stools. As envisioned for this production the structure of the room is as follows: a door leading to the outside world is upstage right, the window through which she dispenses advice to those who come to her is situated stage right; next to that window is a small stool. Downstage center is a window that overlooks her garden and the town of Norwich. Downstage left is her fireplace. Upstage left is an opening leading to another room where her maid had lived. Stage left is another

11

window which looks into the church sanctuary. It is through this window that she receives Communion. Below the stage-left window is her bed. Her chest is stage center and upstage center is her altar. Behind the altar is a small stool.

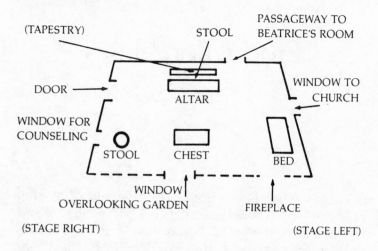

It should be noted that the doors and windows are used in pantomime. They, the fireplace, and the walls do not exist structurally, but are defined by the ingenuity and imagination of the actress.

The bed and altar are defined by the way they are dressed: a straw pallet or blanket for the bed; altar hangings for the altar can be placed over low folding tables. The chest should be real. The tapestry is optional. In this production, it is behind the altar—concealed by a curtain (dossal)—and is revealed near the end of the play. See cartoon at end of book.

PROPERTIES FOR THE PRODUCTION
In keeping with the style of the play, properties are minimal. Some are pantomimed, such as the thread and

needle used by Julian; the cat, Isaiah; putting wood on the fire; feeding of the mouse.

Properties:
1. A priestly stole that Julian sews
2. A bag of clothing which includes children's stockings, a woman's shift, a man's coat
3. A homemade loaf of brown bread
4. A flagon of wine
5. Julian's book
6. The *Anchoresses' Rule* (book)
7. A crucifix on the altar
8. Two candlesticks and holders
9. Two altar vases with flowers (red carnations mixed with spring blooms)
10. Pen (quill) and ink—concealed behind the altar—this is optional as its use can be pantomimed
11. A stool behind the altar used when Julian writes at the altar
12. A small bookstand used when Julian writes (optional)
13. A woolen blanket
14. Taper for lighting the candles
15. Lighted votive candle on altar

Costume for Julian:
1. A basic shift (dress)
2. A gown with a hood, either gray or brown
3. A blue azure mantle (coat)
4. A hazelnut necklace

Sound:
1. Angelus bells
2. Church bells
3. Alto recorders

The poem is broken into two acts with one intermission.

During the intermission, Julian retires behind her altar to write while alto recorders play "Lord of the Dance."

The directorial concept also includes a movement from winter to spring, from Lent to Easter. The play starts with early spring and takes us back into the winters of Julian's experiences with the plagues, her self-doubts, and finally to the Passion of Jesus. In the second act, Julian tells of the horrors of the Peasants' Revolt and the desperation of John Ball's mother. But throughout, the promise of spring and its cleansing, relieving rains, acts as a leitmotiv, ultimately bursting forth in the final moments of the play with the bells of the Resurrection and the uncovering of the tapestry of Christ "suffering in the midst of beauty!"

NOTES ON THE ACTING OF JULIAN

The acting of the play demands an almost Brechtian approach: at times, Julian speaks to the audience. She shares her life, her experiences, her words with them. The audience is her confidante. The style of acting for those moments is presentational and descriptive—and immediate.

Yet as Julian becomes involved with relating her life and happenings, the audience is forgotten as she relives the past. The style of acting becomes representational. In the script, those moments are sometimes introduced by the sound of bells—an almost Proustian device.

Fluidity is of the essence as the actress moves in and out of the two theatrical approaches, but unlike Brecht, who sought to distance the audience in order to teach them, Janda's use of these approaches is to move us, to involve us, to make us understand the Love that was Julian's.

BING D. BILLS

Prologue

This play, Julian, which you are about to see, is a dramatic monologue based on the life and times of Julian of Norwich and her written work, *Revelations of Divine Love*.

Mystic, writer, spiritual guide, Julian is the first-known Englishwoman whose written work survives.

She was born in 1342, two years after Chaucer, and, it is believed, lived well into her seventies.

She was an anchoress, that is, a woman who chose a life of solitude and prayer, and lived in a small two-room apartment adjoining a church. An anchoress was not necessarily a nun.

Julian's anchorhold (or cell) adjoined Saint Julian and Edward Church in Norwich, England, and there she lived and listened to those who would come for spiritual guidance.

Julian was a survivor. She lived through the Hundred Years' War, three outbreaks of the Black Plague which reduced the population of England by half, the violence of the Peasants' Revolt, and the Great Western Schism which brought chaos to all of Christendom.

Another interesting woman of that age was Margery Kempe. She also left us a manuscript, her biography, *The Book of Margery Kempe.*

As the play opens, Julian has been listening to Margery Kempe.

Act I

(As the scene opens, Julian *sits on SR stool, sewing a priestly stole as she continues to listen to* Margery *who is seated SC on chest)*

Yes, Margery, I understand.
There are tempests
and storms,
and howling winds,
and hail and ice,
but they too shall pass—

The Holy Church—a what?

A ship of fools?

But Margery,
if you image it
a ship—

I beg your pardon,
I was not listening?

A "leaking" ship
of fools—

19

Yes, Margery, I have seen
a few fine paintings
depicting it as such—

No—

But—

That is quite true,
none has depicted it
as a "leaking" ship—

You are quite right,
none has done thus—

I?

(She stops sewing and moves SC, sits on chest next to
Margery)

I see it more
as a nest—

Yes, a nest—

No, not a hornet's nest,
a bird's nest,
a robin's nest—

Yes, it was meant to protect
the fledgling soul
until it is ready to fly—

Now who might the mother bird be?

(Julian begins sewing again)

No, not the pope,
nor bishop,
nor priest—

No, none such as me—

Think, Margery, think.
You have seen her pictured—

Close, not the dove,
but whom the dove symbolizes,
God's Holy Spirit—

Yes, I did call the Holy Spirit
"her."

Yes, I know, everybody
is suspected of heresy
these days—

Yes, I am careful.
I'd never say "her" to confuse
a priest or bishop—
only to women such as we—

Yes. That is our joke.

(Margery *has moved DSL to hearth*)
What, leaving so soon?

To see a White Friar?

Who?

Brother Anthony?

Brother Anselm?

Brother Joseph?

You can't recall his name,
but he abides at—

Brother William,
Brother William Sowfeld.

21

He confirms you in your
vow of chastity? But
what of your good husband?

He objected at first, but
has since succumbed to
the Holy Spirit?

But Margery, married life
with husband and children
is not lechery.

You say chastity is a more
perfect way. I beg to disagree—

Did not our Maker
wish such? Seeing as he fashioned us
thusly?

Oh, you have a heaven-sent
confirmation of it?

A stone and piece of
wood beam fell
down from the ceiling
of the church and struck
your back while at prayer—

And you are here to tell of it.

(Julian *puts her sewing down, gets up from chest and moves
to fireplace, to* Margery)

Yes, but what has this
to do with denying your
husband by new vows?

Oh, a sign from God.

You ought to
remain chaste?

(Julian, *attempting to follow* Margery's *logic, crosses up and sits on edge of bed SL*)

Now how does that follow?

I am not tired—
I quite follow you.

Yes, I have seen several
people today.

(Julian *escorts* Margery *to USR door*)

What? Oh, bless you. Bless you
for the wine and bread.

Godspeed, Margery,
Godspeed you, Margery Kempe.

Advice and ghostly counsel!
If I have said fair words,
they come not from me,
but—

From God—
God, our mother.

Yes, Godspeed.

Yes. I shall be careful.

Yes. I know they are burning heretics.

(Margery *leaves.* Julian *closes her door, sighs and crosses DSC to her window and opens it, reflecting on the beauty of God's nature*)

It is still early in the day!

A squirrel.

Squirrels notice
trees budding
before we do.

There she sits
on the long
hanging branch—

sitting there
so surely
on the swaying branch,
chewing
the bud she
just picked;

her tail she uses
as a balance pole
as does an acrobat.

Snowdrops are blooming.
One purple crocus blooms.

(She snaps out of her reverie and addresses the audience)

Forgive me,
I often talk to myself,
but when I do that
I am talking to you
also—am I not?

You know my name,
but I am called
by many names
and many things.

The names I favor:

Julian, Dame Julian,
the ankress at Norwich.

Yes, I am an ankress
and live by the *Anchoresses' Rule.*

(She crosses up to her altar and picks up the book, bringing it down to the window to read)

"Ye shall not possess any beast,
my dear sisters, except a cat."*

And so I have my cat—
Isaiah is his name.

(As she returns the book to the altar, she begins looking for Isaiah)

He does not keep to the cell
as I do,

but then a beast may not choose
as humankind may do:

the beasts, as the flowers,

give praise to God
by simply being,

mankind through choice
with willing, hoping, loving.

(As she finishes her thoughts on her knees after looking under her bed for Isaiah, *she hears a scratching at the door USR, crosses and opens door. It is* Isaiah. *She picks him up, fondly stroking the creature, as she sits SC on chest)*

Isaiah, where is Beatrice?

(She strokes Isaiah, *who is comfortably napping on* Julian's *lap)*

And I have a maid,
she, Beatrice,
now has a home of her own
with two perfect children;

one has deep hazel eyes
and hair like golden wheat,

and the other,
he takes after his father,
a fisherman,
this child has eyes
the color of the sea,

blue green,
and chestnut hair,
soft and fine.

*(*Isaiah, *sufficiently satisfied with* Julian's *stroking, jumps down)*

Beatrice is expecting
a third child.

She brings me all I need;
firewood,
salted flounder,

and fresh milk,
bread which she bakes,
and when she can spare it,
an egg or two.

This room shelters me.
I have my bed and board,
—— hearth and altar.

(Julian *crosses SR above her altar, and points USL*)

Through that door is
the room where Beatrice slept
before she married.

I have three windows;

(*She moves SL to window above her bed*)

through that window,
I hear the Mass
and see the priest at altar,

and the Holy Bread
suspended in a silver dove
above the altar,

and through that window,
only in the morning,
I listen to those
God sends my way.

(Julian *moves to her public window SR and sits to demonstrate her daily work by opening her window*)

In my younger days,
I would see all,
I would welcome all
any time of day,

but I have found
true speech
cannot be
when one is on fire
with drink:

as you may suspect
not all come
with holy intent—

only in the morning
are my shutters open.

So many come—
for spiritual advice
or ghostly counsel,
as they say;

they speak of
pain and loss,
confusion and despair,
fear and death,

the sorrowing,
the sick,
the unwanted,
the lonely,

both young and old,
rich and poor,
all come to my window.

"No one listens,"
they tell me,

and so I listen
and tell them
what they have just
told me,

and I sit in silence
listening to them,
letting them grieve.

"Julian, you are wise,"
they say,
"you have been gifted
with understanding."

All I did was listen.

For I believe full surely
that God's Spirit
is in us all,
giving light, wisdom,
understanding,

speaking words in us
when we cannot speak,

showing us gently
what we would not see,
what we are afraid to see,

so we may show pity,
mercy, forgiveness,
to ourselves.

"There is no creature
that is made

that may wot how much
and how sweetly
and how tenderly
our Maker loveth us—

for he loveth and liketh us
and so willeth he

that we love and like him
and mightily trust in him

and all shall be well."†

(Julian *closes her window, satisfied with her meditation,
moves DSC to look out the window that reveals the gardens
and Norwich beyond*)

And through this window,
I may see—all;

this spring

and another fall
if it be God's will.

Spring and fall,
subtle times;

winter and summer
are so definite,

what is subtle
and indefinite
comforts me—

and Norwich too,

with its apprentices and journeymen,
its farmers, friars, ferrymen,
housewives and children;
travellers, weavers, dyers,
and squealing pigs,

and merchants from Flanders,
Germany, and France trading
fish, blubber,

cloth, gloves,
pepper, wine, and vinegar—

for wool, grease, and livestock;

the beggars, the strikers,
the wandering minstrels.

(Turns and looks at her room)

This room, my anchorhold,
is enough to me.

(Pauses and looks at the audience as if a question had been asked)

My age? Twice that of the Christ—
before he ascended.

(She crosses SL and sits on downstage edge of her bed)

So much has come to pass.

For well over thirty years
I have chosen the solitary life,
and it has been enough to me.

I love solitude.

I rise early to pray,
to welcome God's new day,

and at night I give thanks for all
that has passed;

I use Simeon's prayer:

"Lord,
now lettest thou
thy servant depart in peace,

31

according to thy word:
For mine eyes have seen thy salvation,
Which thou hast prepared
before the face of all people;
A light to lighten the Gentiles,
and the glory of thy people
Israel.''

That is a beautiful way
to end the day,

and to commend to God
sleep and night.

(Julian *gets up and crosses to the altar USC and caresses the* Anchoresses' Rule)

Yes, I live alone
as the *Anchoresses' Rule*
admonishes:

(She finds the precise spot in the book, and moves DSC to window, which she opens)

''Housewifery is Martha's part,
and Mary's part is quietness and rest
from all the world's din,
that nothing may hinder her
from hearing the voice of God.''*

The voice of God,
that has been my wish,
that has been my desire.

(Suddenly an idea comes to her which she must write down. She rushes up to the altar and fetches pen, ink, and her book, which she keeps under her pillow. She proceeds to work out the following poem, seated behind SR side of altar)

"God,
of thy goodness,
give me thyself:

for thou art enough to me,

and I may nothing ask
that is less,

that may be
full worship to thee;

and if I ask anything
that is less,

ever me wanteth,

but only in thee
have I all."†

*(Having finished her poem, she blows on the ink to dry it.
She sees the bag of clothes she offered to mend for Beatrice)*

Oh, but I have my mending to do:
children's clothes,
Beatrice brought them last week,
she has so much to do.

And it is commanded by
the *Anchoresses' Rule:*

"Make no purses, to gain friends therewith,
nor blodbendes of silk;
but shape, and sew, and mend church vestments,
and poor people's clothes."*

(She takes out each item of clothing and tosses it on her bed)

Here are four pairs of stockings,

Beatrice's old shift,
and her good husband's coat—
which smells of fish.

(She sits on bed, threading her needle, and begins to mend a stocking)

"Be never idle . . .
iron that lieth still
soon gathers rust;
water that is not stirred
soon stinketh."*

There is wisdom here.

It was a harsh winter.

Holy Week will be cold . . .
there were light snows
well into spring.
Early this week
the snow fell
as feathers and
covered the dying
drifts with white
lace,

but pasqueflowers
broke through
that seamless snow shroud,
and soon—
briar and brush,
tree and thicket
will break budding
and green.

(The Angelus bells ring three times. She stops her work and

kneels before her altar. The Angelus bells "dissolve" as Julian
gets up and moves DSC to relive the Plague)

Easter, spring, birth—
it is again upon us,

after all those dyings,
after all those deaths,
from the Black Death.

I was but a child
in my sixth year
when it first struck.
I remember the bells
tolling, tolling, tolling.

My good mother tried
to keep us within
to prevent our knowing,

but one morning
I slipped out:

down the road
came John the baker
bearing a bundle—

as he passed,
I saw a child's arm
swaying
out of the sack
clutching
a cloth doll,
and upon the face
of him
who carried the child
was death,

and the bells kept tolling.

There was not consecrated ground
to hold all the dead.

Whole families were taken,

and those with whom
I used to play
I saw no more.

(The tolling bell stops)

Empty homes were
all that was left,
then the bells stopped tolling
for he who tolled the bells
was no more.

Then came a silence:

cottages were empty,
the mill was stilled,

the silence stayed
into fall, into winter.

There were none to
harvest the wheat,
none to harvest
the fruit—apples
and pears lay rotting
around the trees.

There were no priests
to say the mass,
to visit the sick,
to commend to God
the newly dead.

Everywhere there
was mourning—

few had will to live.

Sheep and cattle,
pigs and chickens
wandered through town.

There were none to
pen them in
or gather them into barn
or feed them,

and the silence
was only broken by
wailing

or the wind

or the coughing
of those where
the contagion had
spread.

One could hear the
lowing of lost cattle

or the bleating
of stray sheep

and winter came
with howling winds.

(The tolling of the bell echoes again, as she sits on the chest and begins to immerse herself in the second Plague)

And the Death came again
when I was past twenty.

(She picks up her mending and slowly cradles it as if it were the child)

I was tending a widow's
children;
the youngest, a child
of two, had gotten the Death,
wasted and died.

(The bell stops)

Even after his eyes had
closed, I held him—
I felt the fire of his
fever hours after his death.

I cried loud and long
and though I believed
he was with God,

my mother could not
comfort me.

*(She holds out the "child" to her mother. Julian, feeling the
cold, wraps her cloak tightly about her. Her reverie ends. She
crosses to her fireplace DSL and pantomimes putting wood on
the fire)*

It is chill here.
I must blow the coals
and add wood.

And yet a third time
did the Plague return,
the Death—the Black Death;

and fear ruled,
and despair ruled,
and anger did reign.

Some betook themselves
to the churches

(She crosses to her bed)

> with tears, with praying
> and wailing.

> Many did plead with God
> to take them from this earth,

> and most in anguish
> saw nothing but death:

(She touches clothing of Beatrice's *family)*

> husbands did see
> wives dying

> and wives did see
> their husbands pass,

> children did see
> their mothers dying

> and mothers did see
> their children pass.

> And fear ruled.

(Sitting on the bed, she picks up Beatrice's *shift and uses it to demonstrate the horrors of the Plague)*

> At first a lump appeared
> on the body, the size of an egg,

> then did spots cover the body,
> then came the fever
> with vomiting,
> with coughing,
> then swiftly—death.

> And despair ruled.

(Julian moves DSC to audience)

Mothers abandoned their
children lest they themselves
be contaminated,

the young in fear
abandoned the aged,

husbands fled from their wives,
wives from their husbands,

brother fled brother,
sister parted with sister,

fathers barred the door to sons
and sons cast out infected fathers,

priests abandoned the infected
and physicians, the dying.

And the Death spared none:

neither bishop nor priest,
neither lad nor lass,

neither scholar nor student,
master nor journeyman,

neither merchant nor sailor,
neither artisan nor smith;

young or old,
proud or humble,

all were taken.

Then did despair reign:

there was no herb, no poultice,
neither cordial nor gold,
no balm nor drink,

nothing could prevent the Death.

Then did anger reign:

(She returns to her bed and gathers clothes, clutching them to her bosom as if they were all humanity)

there was the howling
and cursing,
many shouted blasphemies
and cursed the day their
mothers bore them,

then did many curse God,

then all gave way to silence.

(She slowly drops the individual pieces of clothing into the bag by the altar)

The howls and cursing ceased,
the cries of pain and anguish ceased,
the blasphemies ceased,

all gave way to silence.

(Julian puts hood over head as she moves SR to stool and sits with her back to the audience)

Winter came.
The earth was dumb.

We who lived on
were dumb,
we waited in silence,

we waited in the
cold and dark,

we waited for
the thawing,

and though neither lips
nor tongue
could form words,

(She turns to the audience slowly)

our hearts felt a warmth,
a gratitude and quiet praise

for the life we had been given,
for our lives that had been spared.

(She takes her hood off and comes DSC)

And as for me in all this silence
I suffered from
noise, voices
in my head.

Often I could not sleep.

Accusing voices
endlessly telling me
that I was responsible
for all the evil
and suffering in England.

At times I could
not hear my self
or anyone else—

it was as if
I were judge,
jury, attorney,
and condemned—

I could not defend
my helpless self—

there were none
to defend me—

and I began to hate
my self—

the voices, the accusing
condemning voices—

they grew louder
and louder till

I cried out to God
that he in his mercy
would give me peace—
to live,
to stop the voices.

God heard my cries,

the voices gave way
to silence—

the madness ended,
for I was shown
the suffering Christ,
the forgiving Christ,

and that has made
the difference.

It was an understanding,
a deep understanding.

How do I find words
to tell of it?

(Crosses to bed to get her book, sits and tries to find passage

where she expressed her ideas—instead, she closes book and explains)

And with the understanding
I could acknowledge
my fear, my terror,
my anger, my helplessness,
my ignorance, my confusion—

it was as if I could
forgive myself
and every other

because I felt in my heart
God had forgiven me,

I could now stop my
self-hating,
my blaming,

and turn my life
to simple tasks
which make for peace—

my own—and others—

and see, for the first time,
the good in all—

and see God in all.

(Julian drops to the floor, pauses with her hands on the ground, and slowly comes to a standing position)

Grounded
in
God where
only
mercy and

truth
can grow

neither
wrath
nor anger
root
here nor

blame to
us
who slowly
grow

in a medley
of
weal and woe

in him who
is
ever meek
ever
mild who

wakes us
from
desperate
sleeps
with the
touch
of a child

he our
bloodroot
flower.

The Death had passed.

(She puts her book back on bed, suddenly turns and addresses audience)

You are here—I also,
this seemeth me
cause for rejoicing.

*(She moves to SR of altar, crosses herself and eats and drinks
from the bread and wine* Margery *had left. She removes a
little of the bread to feed Moses the mouse later in the play)*

Listen.

Birds sing.

Cedar and shrub
gleam
with raindrops.

There is a freshness
in the air

and a quickness in
these old bones.

(She opens USR door and looks out)

Pigeons flap past
and
sparrows chatter and
scold
in the eaves
of
Saint Julian and Edward
Church.

Behold it all.

*(*Isaiah *enters)*

Isaiah does;

(She sees her cat seated in the DSC window, comes to him and looks out)

> he sits at the window
> listening and looking,
> watching,
> his tail gives lie
> to his interior peace.
>
> In wood and hill
> swollen streams
> rush with melted snow
> and spring rain.
>
> It is raining now.

(She puts her hand out to feel the rain)

> Everything is being
> bathed, washed—
>
> you can hear the rain
> splashing off the eaves,
>
> the fat drops are the
> size of herring scales,
>
> there is a smell
> of wet earth
> in the cool air,
>
> a mother robin
> is nested
> in the hawthorn,

(She leans out window to better see the robin)

she is brooding
with
wings spread
over the
nest,

rain rolls off
her wings,

she is warming
the new life,
the shelled promise.

"God is all that is good,
as to my sight,
and the goodness
that everything hath,
it is he."†

And the Christ,
he came to make
all things new,

and his death,
it was for love:

the cruel scourging,
the mocking,
the hurtful crowning—

for love.

It runs plenteously
as
rain off the eaves

*(She holds out her hands, catching the rain, and then splashes
the water on her face gently. She then beholds the water in
her hands as if it had become the blood of Christ)*

splashing, bathing,
washing, increasing

all life that is—

this rain becoming
all that it loves and
keeps in its making

the blood of Christ—

beyond our wit
the
force of its flowing
its
never beginning
its
never ending

with promise of
springs
fresh full and
flowering
as sea froth the
blossoming

(She stares at her hands and slowly extends them outwards)

must be our dying
must be our dying.

I almost died.

"When I was thirty years old
and a half
God sent me a bodily sickness
in which I lay

three days and three nights."†

I quite sincerely wanted
to be ill,
that was my desire.

This desire
came not of despair,
no—rather—
it came of love:

the seed was faith,
the root, a desire
for understanding,
the shoot, compassion,

the blossom—
to understand,

to stand under
his pain to know
his love

as did his good
mother,
as did the Magdalen,
and John,
his true lovers

who stood by him
at the cross.

I would be
oned
with them

in their sorrow
and grief,
in their pain
and contrition.

I would be oned
with them,

to be there with them
before my dying Maker—

to see with mine
own eyes

his pain
that I might understand
his love.

(She moves DSL continuing to address the audience)

Yes, my fellows,
such were
my desires—

and all these desires,
each one of them,
has been granted.

And so I prayed
that after I was thirty
(not before)

that—that I might pass
through a sickness
unto death,
yet be spared,
yet live.

I desired all the pain,
all the fears,
all the assaults
of the demons which

I had seen

so many others
pass through,

that I might live
more fully for him
who had lived and
died so fully for me,

for I felt full surely
that in our last agony,
in our final suffering,
in our dying—

will be the last
act of loving,
of believing,
of hoping.

Yes, that desire was granted—

(She moves the chest back up against the altar as she prepares to relate part of her Visions)

when I was thirty and a half:

(As Julian *begins the story she removes her outer cloak and forms it into a pillow, placing it under her arm. She crosses to the bed)*

I lay for three days
in the throes of death;

I could not breathe—
such was my shortness
of breath,

and so great were
my pains,

I doubted not
that I should
soon die.

(She pantomimes the placing of the pillow on the bed)

Those about me
pulled me up in bed,
and with pillows
sat me,
that I might breathe
more freely.

(She moves to chest and places her cloak on it. She then removes the cross from the altar and kisses the five wounds of the Crucified. Having done so, she then places cross on altar)

On the fourth night,
I took all my rites of Holy Church
and thought not to have
lived till day.

I was dead from
the middle down,

I could not feel my legs;

(Standing by the chest in front of altar, she gestures towards SR door where curate had entered)

My curate was sent for
to be at my ending.

I heard my mother
weeping—
and pleading with me

53

to live,

but could make
her no answer.

*(She picks up the altar cross and moves it slowly until it is
in front of her)*

He—my curate—
came and setting the cross
before my face, said,

"I have brought thee the image
of thy Maker and Saviour,

look thereupon
and comfort thee
therewith."†

*(She places the cross on the floor next to the chest as she
sits on it, transforming it into a bed)*

Then my sight
began to fail
and in my sleep—

(She screams. In the following section, Julian *at times addresses the audience; at other moments she is reliving her battle
with the fiend. All of this occurs as she is seated on the chest)*

I saw the devil.

I felt the fiend
had me
by the throat

putting his foul face
so close

54

I could see black spots
like freckles
all about his
filthy face.

It was red
as a tilestone
newly fired

as was his hair
hanging over his
greasy face,
speckled with soot.

With his sly grinning
I saw his white teeth,

and with his paws—
they were no human hands—
I thought he would
choke me to death.

I cried out.

Those about me
with cool rags did
bathe my forehead.

I could feel their
hands holding me down.

I reasoned they must not
be seeing
what I was seeing
and yet I was seeing
a suffocating smoke
billowing through the door;
I was feeling a great heat
and smelling a sickening stench.

In my terror,
I again cried out.

(Julian *rises from her bed and rushes DSC, still transfixed
by her story. She cries out with arms extended*)

"Benedicite, Domino,"

for I thought
the whole place
was on fire.

I was gasping
for breath.

"See ye not hell?
Smell ye not the stench?
Know ye not the fiend?"

(*She moves backwards to the chest*)

"No, no, no,"
I heard them saying.

"Oh God help me,"
I shouted—

(*She sits in terror and reaches for the crucifix, holding it
before her. She rises, using the crucifix to banish the fiend*)

for I knew
it was the fiend
who had come to tempt me
with terror—

which terror in God's eye
is no thing—nothing.

Then it all vanished.

(She sits on chest, clutching the crucifix to her. As she once again gazes at it, suddenly she sees the Vision of her crucified Jesus in front of her)

There was darkness
all about me
as if it had been night,

save in the image
of the cross
whereon I beheld
a gentle light,

and in that
halo of light

I looked upon
my Maker—

my gentle, courteous,
helpless, dying Maker.

I beheld the face
of my Saviour.

The red blood
was flowing

down his gentle face,
down from under
the thorns.

(Drawn by the suffering of the Christ, she rises and moves DSL to share in his torture)

Great drops of blood
as fat beads
were forming,
forming and flowing

down that sacred face,
down that innocent face,
down his helpless face.

Forming and flowing
forming and flowing,

falling as rain;
heavy drops of rain that
fall from the eaves,

as rain drenching leaves,

as rain steaming on cold earth,
loosening the hard and frozen earth.

And in that rain,
and in his face,

I saw all that is helpless;

the blinking eyes of the wounded bird,
the terror of the snared hare,
the fear of the dying wounded hart,
the trampled rose.

And the great drops
of blood oozed brown red,
swelling into beads
and breaking and spreading,
crimson red, scarlet red,

trickling down,
clotting at the eyebrows.

(Unable to bear the horror, she moves backwards to the chest and sits, numbed by the Vision)

Down, down his holy face
did this heavy rain continue—

falling, falling, falling.

I believed the very sheets of my
deathbed would be soaked
in scarlet red.

And I continued to look upon
that face
as I felt hot tears
and my heart swelling—

for in that face
I saw the face of all
that is wounded,
all that is suffering;

the lost child,
the mocked mute,
the withered mother
with no more milk
to give.

I felt my heart would
break with grief,

I felt I could be shown
no more,

but he did look
upon me
and said,

*(She kneels in front of her chest, clutching the crucifix as
she hears the words of her Lord)*

"My darling,

I have embraced
your pain,

it is part of
my pain,

when you suffer,
I suffer.

My blood rain
is watering

your roots.

I am every man,
I am every thing.

You are me
and we

are all one.

I am your mother
putting

herself in debt
to you

wishing none come
ever

to grief

by suffering
by dying

at other hands

for your sake.

I love you
more than
my life itself.

Know,
my daughter,

know

that I would
die
ten thousand
times
if thou wouldst
but believe."

With such words
did he
comfort me—

for he willed
that I see more
of his suffering
near the time
of his dying.

And I did see.

*(She rises, moves DSL, leaving the crucifix on the chest.
She wishes to be nearer her Saviour)*

Slowly did his
bleeding cease—

and—and his dear face
did lose its color
for the hue of death
was upon him.

In my grief,
in my helplessness,

I prayed his death
be quick;
so hurtful to me
was his suffering,

and yet for some time
did he live
fixed to that cross.

(She now stands beneath the cross in her Vision)

He grew cold and
withered.

His body did sag forward
for his flesh and bones
and sinews
could no longer sustain
his body weight.

His wounds gaped,
his body fell forward
under its own weight.

I could not ease
his pain—

I closed my eyes
and looked away—

I besought the Father
to deliver him up to death
for his pain became my pain.

(She extends her arms—fingers extended in pain, eyes closed)

And when I felt
I could no more,

and when I cried,
"I can no more,"

I looked upon him
one last time

pleading with the Father
to forgive me,

when suddenly,

(Slowly begins to relax her arms)

his countenance
did change

from pain to
blissful cheer—to joy!

yet I could not doubt
that I did see or
what I did see;

he was right glad
and merry,

and he did laugh:

and I did laugh.

"Where now is any point
of thy pain or grief?"
said he.

(Alto recorders: "Lord of the Dance" beginning softly and building. She reaches out as if to help Jesus down from the cross)

"There is no pain in earth
or in any other place
that should aggrieve thee.

(She is embraced by Jesus)

Lo, how I love thee.

Now is all my bitter pain
and all my hard travail
turned to endless joy
and bliss.

(Her arms opened wide)

See, I am God:
see, I am in all thing:
see, I do all thing:
see, I lift never mine hands off my works,
nor ever shall, without end:

(Julian moves as if led by Jesus DSL)

see, I lead all thing to the end
I ordained it to be
from without beginning,
by the same Might, Wisdom, and Love
whereby I made it.

How should anything be amiss?"†

(Music stops. The Vision disappears. For a moment she
remains transfigured. In joy she crosses DSC and shares her
understanding with the audience)

This flesh,
our birthing,
living,
dying flesh
which so hampers us,
that so pulls us down—

the Son of God,
our Saviour,
took on himself!

Ah, it is but
Adam's old coat—
so tight,
so threadbare,
too short,

this,

(She goes behind altar and puts on a blue mantle)

our Saviour
takes and
cuts and shapes
into a handsome
cloak
warm and flowing
and full—

blue as the sky,
God's eye,

azure as the ocean,
clear as lake and stream:
each is his dream.

(She then takes the crucifix and places it back on the altar)

Yes, we are his crown,
his delight, his endless bliss.
How God is rejoicing
to be our Father.

(She places vase of flowers on altar)

How God is rejoicing
to be our Mother.

(Second vase of flowers is put in place)

He shows us
what he is—

the motherhood
of mercy—

(She lights a taper from the votive candle and then lights the first altar candle)

pushing each of us
out of her darkness

(She lights second altar candle)

into a world of light
and opening her arms
to us—to each—
her ever children.

Oh, our human mother
tenderly offers her breast,

"but our tender Mother, Jesus,"
leads us to his breast
through his open side

and into his heart
that we may know
true joy,
true gladness,
heavenly bliss.

(She picks up Margery's *gifts of bread and wine from the altar)*

With love,
with courtesy

our Mother feeds us
with herself,

the blessed Sacrament,
precious food,

*(She crosses down from behind the altar and gives the bread
to a member of the audience)*

the bread and wine
of all true life.

"Take, eat—"

he gives
his selfbread
to become us

and begs only belief
is his hunger
us to hallow.

(She gives the wine to another member of the audience)

"Drink my blood wine,
and know I would die
a thousand deaths for you,

for I give you my promise,
sealed in blood,

I shall not leave you orphans."

*(*Julian *retires behind her altar to write. During the Intermission, alto recorders play "Lord of the Dance")*

INTERMISSION

Act II

(At the end of the Intermission Julian *puts out the candles on the altar and then takes up her book and begins to write the following)*

"Some of us believe that God
is Almighty and may do all,

and that he is All-Wisdom
and can do all;

but that he is All-Love
and will do all,

there we stop short."†

(Pause)

Silence—how dear it is,
where may one find it?

a quiet place,
a place to dwell alone?

Here? One would think so,
but, not always—

(Comes DSC to tell us the story)

just yesterday,
after the gospel,

(She goes to the church window SL)

there was such shouting
and joke making,

I could not hear
the good priest

as he said the words
making bread and wine
Christ's body and blood.

(She pantomimes the following story)

I looked up to see William,
the butcher's son,
dripping hot wax from his candle
down from the upper stall
onto the bald head
of Henry the feltmaker
below.

(She crosses DSL to audience)

It even behooved a certain bishop
to legislate against
wrestling and stone throwing
here—during Mass—
not too long past.

(Crosses back and sits on chest and sews)

But Jesus, he would have been
at home here.

He chose simple fishermen—
not in wood and stone
does he dwell
but in our soul.

(Crosses to bed, picks up her book and comes back to DSC window and reads)

"The place that Jesus taketh in our Soul
he shall never remove it,
without end, as to my sight;
for in us is his homliest home
and his endless dwelling."†

(She closes her book, clasping it to her bosom, and looks out DSC window)

Crocuses—can you see them?
And a clump of snowdrops? so delicate.

It comes so gently,
spring,
that's how God touches us,
so gently,
as spring—or as a father,
a father with his firstborn.

The mother knows no fear
in picking up the child
and nursing it,

but the father,
he is afraid.

He must be coaxed
to do it.

God our Father loves us
full tenderly
as a firstborn—

at times,
I think he
is afraid of us.

(She crosses to bed and puts her book down, and then looks through window above bed)

Sometimes,
I cannot sit still
at sermon time:

one would think
the priest had the holy oils
poured on him
to preach hate.

God does not hate,
God cannot hate,
God will not hate,
what he has made.

(Julian moves across room and ends up DSR as she addresses the audience)

We are his children.

God said to the prophet, Isaiah,

"Can a mother leave
her baby at the breast?

Can she throw her child

out of her heart?

Even if she could,
I will never forsake you."

And Jesus said,

"My people, my people,
if only you would let me
gather you under my wings
as a hen does her chicks—"

That is Jesus speaking,
Jesus our Mother.

As truly as we receive
our flesh and blood
from our mother,

as truly as we are made
of our mother's body,

as truly as her body
is earth and shall
return to earth,

so truly has the earth
been made by God
who is in every sense
our Mother.

(She moves DSL)

That is the reasoning
I used with a visiting theologian,
a very learned man—
I will not tell his name.

"Dame Julian," said he,
"how can ye call
the Christ our Mother?"

(She crosses to stool by window SR)

And so I had to show him
how God spoke as mother
in Holy Writ.

(As she sits, she makes the "Sign of the Cross" on her mouth, ears, eyes, and breast, and then proceeds)

"It is but a woman's way,"
I said:

"He that is so tender
and loveth us so much,
is not this
the mother's part?

And he that hath made
both man and woman,
doth he not possess
the qualities of each?

as song is in the bird?

or as in the seed
is hidden
the flower's color?

Is not tenderness and womankind
hidden in our Creator?

And in thee, God's priest,
is there not tenderness?

I say Christ our Mother
because it is the mother
who best shows love,

as the flower shows color
and the sea and storm—power.

76

It is but an image,
for how else may we speak?

How else put what is
inside—outside?"

He reluctantly agreed,
but bid me hold my tongue—

got up, made for the door—
stepping on Isaiah's tail.

(Isaiah *rubs against* Julian's *gown*)

Isaiah? You remember,
don't you?

I must let Isaiah out.

(*She crosses to USR door and lets* Isaiah *out*)

There, out you go.

(*Closes door and crosses DSR and conspiratorially takes the
audience into her confidence*)

And now, I may feed
Moses, Moses the mouse.

(*She takes the bread she saved from the first act and entices*
Moses *out of his hole behind the altar, leading him DSC as
she does so*)

He joined me last fall;
he comes out
for crumbs
which I feed him
only when Isaiah is out.

(She drops some crumbs)

> He is so shy and courteous;
> he humbly accepts every
> crumb and kernel I give him.
>
> And he is so delicate,
> he is so fragile,
> no match for Isaiah.

(She reaches down to touch him gently with one finger, whereupon he scampers back to his "home" behind the altar. Julian follows him up behind the altar)

> Moses is so small,
> so beautiful.
>
> All life,
> all that is,
>
> is good,
> is beautiful.

(Crosses USR, opens door and sees young Tom, waves to him)

> Hello, Tom.
>
> That is Tom, the baker's son.
> He is only eight years old.
> He is carrying bread to the
> widow on King's Street.
>
> There is a cool freshness
> to this late gray spring day.
>
> Colors seem stronger,
> flowers are blossoming—
> their shapes:

bells, stars, lace.

Rain water is running
down the street;

(She leans out to see it)

one dog and three sparrows
are drinking there.

The sparrow—

his is
the task

to sing
in
the city

without
a
country
re-
spite
or
foreign
tour

winters
with
crumbs
are
his fare

though
un-
doubtedly
he
hears chanting

from
the eaves

and with

spring
is
ecstatic
in
petal showers
as
well as
in
colors
of
cultivated
flowers

to say
nothing
of the

luxury
of
cake crumbs
at
weddings

he is cited
by
Christ for

his trust

the Christ
who
never al-
luded
to peacocks

though he
must
have seen them.

Sparrows, pigeons,
dogs and cats,

all gifts from
our loving Maker.

How he must love us
to do thus
without end.

(She crosses up to flowers on the altar)

Birth.

We are reborn
with each birth,
with each spring.

The song of
woods

in all new
leaves

(and before—even
in

the seed) his
hand

tracing oh so
gently

what was already
there

(She takes flower from the vase SR and holds it up to the light)

the veining of
leaves

that thread
ribbing

even on dragonfly
wings

like lead lines
in
rose windows

and Christ light

showing we are
what

he was—God's
image

giving time and
space

for the choosing
of colors.

(With flower in hand, she comes DSC and talks to audience)

See the flowers,
the city faces,
they never end,

like love
they are always beginning,
never ending.

No more than closing the eyes
can stop the pear tree from
blossoming, can love be stopped.

Love is like that,
the Christ is like that,

we may close our eyes
but he is always here
within and without.

He simply cannot
break troth with us.

He is largeness,
he is largesse,
he is bounty,

and the goodness that
every thing hath,
it is he.

"Wit it well:
love is his meaning."†

(She gives the flower to a member of the audience)

Spring with all its
freshness is upon us,

but this spring
shall pass to summer

and thence
to fall,

(She brings her stool DSC and sits to share her thoughts with the audience)

fall with all
its bright leaves
and berries,

a season of husks,

nuts, and shells,
and squirrels
storing food
against winter,

a season of sweet
bird song
and bees
passing from flower
to flower

a season of woods
fringed with
late-blooming asters
and tangles
of weed of sharp
fragrance,

a season of drying herbs;
sage, mint, parsley,
rosemary, thyme,

a season of honeycombs,
quince, winter apples,

a season of ingathering.

Fall is a time of crushings
for wines and ciders,

a time of coopers and carpenters,
wood shavings and oak barrels,

a time of stooks and stalks,
haystacks, sacks of grain,
of field mice and crickets,

fall is nature's pageant,
its crowning carnival,

a rich earth tapestry,

the weavers, the dyers,
the colored yarns,
stained-glass windows,

dusty market places,
parrots, minstrels,
acrobats, hounds,
and hawks,

the buyers, the sellers,
the parents, the children,
the lovers,

the spices; cinnamon,
pepper, camomile, cloves,

a time of peaceful streams
with ducks and geese
floating in red, orange,
and green of reflected
tree colors,

a time of quiet churches,
of dark churches
with windows ablaze
with jeweled light,

and stone pavements
softened with color
from rose windows,

a time of warmth
and evening prayer,

the smell of fish,
roast fowl,
baked bread,
of smoke from
cooking chimneys,

the closing of doors,
the crying of children
put early to bed,

the night, the moon,
the stars, sleep,
and peace.

I must walk a bit,
my bones grow stiff
if I sit too long.

(She stands and moves her stool back to SR position)

Yes, I have walked
this earth for sixty-five years
and I will keep walking
as long as I have life left.

Why are we here?

(Taking the audience once more into her confidence, she comes DSC)

Why am I here?

I should have been dead
and buried at thirty,

and many times since.

That peace—
I think I have found it.

The voice of God—
I think I have heard it.

Mine only enemies,
impatience and despair,
but neither can prevail,

I have learned to laugh—

and the Lord showed me
I would sin.

And I have defined my arrogance:
the nonacceptance
of mine own insignificance—
my foolishness, selfishness, weakness—
strength.

Rocks, hills, and trees
have taught me that;

they were here before
I was born—

(She now moves her chest back to middle of room. She hears the sound of pebbles being thrown against the outer window)

Stones.

(She crosses DSC to her window)

Pebbles have become
a ritual—

some children
known only to me
pelt my window
with pebbles
about this time
occasionally.

I beg your endurance.

I must now
go to my window,
look around,

scowl,
then mutter:

(She does this)

Some people have
nothing better to do
than throw pebbles.

They ought to be
spanked.

I'll soon find out
who they are.

Of course, I know
who they are.

I'll not say a word,
it is innocent play.

Play is pretending
you do not know
when you do know,

it is a medicine
against arrogance,

also despair and
discouragement.

They wanted to
be recognized,

often children
are not.

Discouragement
and despair
are felt when
one has not known

love.

I had to learn this.

Years ago,
the first child
I caught throwing pebbles,
I dealt with harshly.

(She pantomimes the following story)

I took the child
by the collar
and said,

"Tell me it was you
who sent that
shower of stones."

"If I do,
will you yet
love me?"
it asked.

Will you yet
love me—

We cannot admit
to truth
if we feel love
will be lost
or denied.

How children need love.
How all need love.

When one is not loved,
one can only feel
discouragement, despair,
and terror.

And I have felt terror—
with the Peasants' Revolt,
madness reigned.

(Julian *sits on chest SC*)

I was afraid to
leave my room,

it was not safe
to be out on the
streets,

there were murders, beatings,
lootings: brutal behaviour—

half of London was burned
to the ground.

The peasants broke open the prisons
and let condemned murderers escape—

they roamed the streets
and stopped at nothing—

they even murdered the Archbishop
of Canterbury and would have
killed the King himself had not
the Mayor surrounded them and
hemmed them in—

hardly was there a street
without bodies of the slain—

yet part of the
understanding
was that this vision
was not given
for me to keep,

but to share with all
who suffer—

yes, I chose this life
of solitude

to listen and to receive
those God would send to me
for healing,

and they did come.

(She crosses to door USR)

One came ranting
and raving,

cursing and foul-
smelling,

tearing her hair
in anger, in rage,

(Crosses DSR)

her son, the priest,
John Ball,
had been hanged,
drawn,
and quartered—

for leading the peasants
in the uprising,

the bloody pieces of his body
were carried to four points
in the kingdom—as a warning
to those who would break
the common peace.

(She moves up behind altar and relives the story)

"Johnny, Johnny, Johnny,

damn the Bishop
who anointed you,

(She, now as John Ball's mother, upsets candlestick—an act of desecration follows)

and damn the judge
who hanged you,

(Turns over second candlestick)

damn the King
who cared not for
the poor,"

(She takes flower—red carnation—from vase and crushes the blood-red petals above her head)

she cursed in a rage
and I listened.

(She keeps her hands locked above her head as petals fall from her hands)

"I curse the false friends
who abandoned you,

and I curse the clerics
who'd not defend you,

and I curse the fat monks
who cared not a turd for you,"

and I listened.

(She then places altar crucifix upside down)

"Cursed be God
who made me heavy
with you,

cursed be thy father
who played with me
to beget you,

and damned be them
that butchered you
as a filthy hog."

What could I do,
but listen.

"They have made sausage
of my son's body
and are selling it in London
a ha'penny a pound.

I tried to boil it,
but could not.

(Carrying the crucifix upside down, she comes from behind altar and crosses to Julian's *stool SR and kneels, offering* Julian *the crucifix)*

Dame Julian,

for Christ's blood's sake,
pray, Lady Julian, pray—
I do not wish to take
my life—that is a sin.

There is a war
in my head,
a din in my ears,

demons in my marrow.

All I see, is his
bleeding, butchered
body—help me."

(Julian *slowly returns to herself and in mime puts the crucifix on her stool upright and then raises the dazed woman, leading her to the bed SL*)

"Stay, good woman, stay,"
said I,
"There is room for
you here—

(Julian *puts blanket around the broken woman*)

lie down—look,
here is a bed—
and a warm wool blanket.

Rest now.

Listen,
it is raining,

The rain is falling
on the roof.

I will open
the window,

(Julian *crosses SC and opens window*)

hear the rain
gurgling
in the gutters,

it is falling off

the eaves

splashing onto the
street below;

hear the rain tapping on
the leaves,

(She catches rain in her hand and brings it to the bed to soothe the woman's face)

it is washing,
cleansing,
cooling,
calming,

giving drink
to the
thirsting earth,

healing the
parched land.

When you wake—

What?

(She looks at cat, coming out from under the bed)

No, Isaiah will
not harm you—

In the morning
there will be
hot chicken broth
and fresh baked bread."

(She sits on chest, keeping vigil)

And she fell asleep
that night, soundly—

I watched her sleep,
she seemed a child
in her mother's arms.

She stayed with me
for a time—

at first, she did
sleep late,

but as she grew
in strength,

in the mornings,
we would rise early
to pray,

to hear the Mass,

and receive Christ's
body and blood
through that window.

(Sits on chest)

During the heat
of the day

we would sew
and mend

and I would listen
to all
that she would say.

In the evening,
we would sit together
in silence.

(She turns to look at the woman in her bed)

And while she did sleep,
it was given to me to see

that just as every mother
is more minded
of her dying child
than of its survivors,

so too would God
our Mother
embrace and cleave to
that wretched woman

and with a mother-love
keep her full surely,

(She crosses to the bed)

for in that broken
woman lay a good will,
God will—

a good will, God will
that sought to love
and be loved—

and I reasoned
that if she
hurt herself at all—

for that is sin,
self-hurt—

all would be forgiven
if she did but ask,

(She crosses to front of altar)

and she did ask;

"Dame Julian,

for Christ's blood's sake,
pray, Lady Julian, pray,

I do not wish to take
my life—I know that is a sin."

Little by little
her cursing ceased,

slowly, the war in her head
did cease,

and the din in her ears
gave way to silence
and a cheerful peace.

(She crosses DSC to the window)

Then one day she looked
out that window,
turned and said,

"Dame Julian,

I must leave your nest,
I feel I can fly."

I helped her
gather her few
belongings,

a new shift
she had made

and a warm wool cloak
I did not need.

(Julian *walks the woman to the door USR, opens it; they* *embrace*)

> "Lady Julian,
> you are the first
> creature
> that ever loved me,"
> said she, then left.

(Julian *closes door*)

> She never came again.
>
> The kind priest
> that brought her
> to me—returned again.
>
> He told me she was
> now roaming the streets
> of London—begging,
>
> crying, "Peace,
> peace to all,"
>
> and though many
> thought she had lost
> her wits,
>
> I knew that
> she had found
> her soul—
>
> and that,
> none could take
> from her—
> or ever remove.

(*She comes DSR*)

This?

(She points to the hazelnut ornament around her neck)

A fair chain, is it not?
On it hangs
a finely wrought hazelnut
fashioned in silver.

Yes, she put it about my neck
the first week she stayed—
in payment, for the charity.

I knew it was all
she possessed—

to return it,
would be to
humiliate her—

it is so difficult
to give
or receive,
is it not?

(She crosses to bed and folds the blanket she had used for John Ball's mother)

> Her father was a silversmith
> before the Plague
> took him.

(As she speaks, she continues her housekeeping; she goes to altar and scoops up the red petals from the broken flower)

> Who know the deepest
> pain
> taste the deepest joy
> if they
> choose to love—not hate—
> if they choose to live,
> to forgive:
>
> the suffering Christ
> hidden in all—

(She returns the crucifix to the altar. In silence she crosses down to her window SC)

> The suffering.

(She throws petals out of one hand)

> The agony.

(She throws petals from the other hand. She returns to altar and from behind it lights the candles again)

> Agony
>
> may confer

                    a
                    dignity

(First candle is lighted)

                    a majesty
                    with-
                    out livery

(Second candle is lighted)

                        and a void
                        which
                        can contain

                        all—as the
                        eye
                        which knows

                        no surfeit
                        nor
                        alters

                        what it
                        may
                        embrace—

(She bends altar crucifix towards her and gazes lovingly at it)

                        the open
                        hands
                        nailed for

                        Truth's sake

                        with nudity
                        for

privacy as

of the Christ

this wounding
is
for healing

now the
hands
raise only

to cherish
to bless
to praise.

Yes, this age is passing
and I have life left.

(She remains in meditation, holding the arms of the altar crucifix)

A linchpin
an axle

what is needed

is some
center

on which
to turn

oh Christ
more

than my
axis

you are the
warp

of my
tapestry

I want
to weave

my life
with

color threads
of

meadows and
trees

and silver
and gold

against the
night

you also
create.

(She gently stands the cross upright on the altar)

But this age shall pass,
it is passing.

(If the optional tapestry behind the altar is used, she goes to it and slowly removes the veil that has covered a depiction of the crucified Christ surrounded by the beauty of God's world. As she does this, the bells of the Resurrection are rung joyously. Julian then moves down to front of altar, crosses herself, and kneels in meditation. She then describes the tapestry)

This age, my age,
it is a fair tapestry:

in its center

is the Crucified
bleeding in agony
surrounded by trees;

suffering in the
midst of beauty:

the loving Christ
surrounded by trees
of oak and holly;

there are birds in flight,
rabbits, pheasants, and
every kind of fowl near
a splashing stream,

in the distance
is a fair city—

we have suffered
in the midst
of beauty.

*(Having finished her meditation, she rises and comes down
once more to speak with the audience)*

Life
is a precious thing
to me

and a little thing:

my life is a little thing,
when it will end here
is God's secret.

And the world
is a little thing,

like a hazelnut

in his—her hand—

but it is in his ever-keeping,
it is in his ever-loving,
it is in his ever-making,

how should any thing be amiss?

Yes, all shall be well,
and all will be well,
"and thou shalt see thyself
that all manner of thing
shall be well."†

Kind friends,

I pray God grant you
all your good wishes,
desires, and dreams—

it is all in the choosing,

*(She turns and starts to exit USL. She stops and smilingly
turns to the audience to deliver the final line of Julian)*

it is all in the asking.

(FINIS)

106

Each square of the above grid equals ½ foot of the full-scale tapestry.
For a detailed description of the trapestry, see p. 108.

The tapestry used in the original production of **Julian** *was painted with acrylics on a 4' × 6½' pre-gessoed, pre-stretched canvas.*

The color scheme is largely taken from the Unicorn Tapestries in The Cloisters Museum of New York City. The background of the tapestry is a deep forest green. The oak and holly trees are rendered in lighter shades of green, ranging from blue-green to yellow-green.

The outer band of the cross is bright red; the color flows from the hands of the Christ figure. The inner band is gold. The halo is gold, painted on top of a red under-coat to give it more warmth. The color of the inner cross is royal blue, and the Hebrew letters above the cross are turquoise blue.

The colors of the barn swallow, humming bird, ring-necked pheasant, rabbit, and butterflies accord with reproductions found in various texts about wildlife.

The waves of water beneath the feet of the Christ figure are shades of sky blue. Below the waves are forget-me-not blossoms in pale blue.

The wish bones are bone-colored and the "pearls of great price" are ivory. The v-shaped clumps of foliage are yellow-green; the roses are pink; the peaches are their natural, ripened color; the columbine wreath is blue-green.

The mountains are shades of blue, moving from dark blue at the lowest range to light blue at the top range. The sky is very light blue-gray and the moon is white. The castle is a very milky terra-cotta, with indian red towers and pale orange flags. The bushes along the horizon are yellow-green.

At the top left are wild golden daisies, next to white buttercup wild flowers. Above the rabbit's tail are three purple gentian. The kinnikinnick below the rabbit's feet is a glossy, round-leafed green plant with red-orange berries.

The fringe at the bottom of the tapestry is gold.

Of Related Interest

ENFOLDED IN LOVE:
Daily Readings with Julian of Norwich.
96 pages. In paper.
The Seabury Press.